BILLIONAIRE
HUMAN

HOW TO FEEL, NEED AND EXPRESS YOUR SUCCESS

Copyright © 2020 Simon Peter Rosenberg

BILLIONAIRE HUMAN

All rights reserved. No part of this publication may be reproduced, distributed, or transmitted in any form or by any means, including photocopying, recording, or other electronic or mechanical methods, without the prior written permission of the publisher, except in the case of brief quotations embodied in critical reviews and certain other noncommercial uses permitted by copyright law. For permission requests, write to the publisher, addressed "Attention: Permissions Coordinator," at info@beyondpublishing.net

Quantity sales special discounts are available on quantity purchases by corporations, associations, and others. For details, contact the publisher at the address above.

Orders by U.S. trade bookstores and wholesalers. Email info@BeyondPublishing.net

The Beyond Publishing Speakers Bureau can bring authors to your live event. For more information or to book an event contact the Beyond Publishing Speakers Bureau speak@BeyondPublishing.net

The Author can be reached directly at MillioniareHuman.com, GoLoFlix.com, and SimonRosenberg.online

Manufactured and printed in the United States of America distributed globally by BeyondPublishing.net

New York | Los Angeles | London | Sydney

ISBN Paperback: 978-1-952884-00-9

ISBN epub: 978-1-952884-04-7

ISBN Hardcover: 978-1-952884-85-6

Editor's Note: Some words are intentionally capitalized for emphasis

FÜR TAMARA

Die Schönheit und Sanftheit deiner Liebe zeigt mir den Weg zum Leben und öffnet mir Fenster und Türen zu einem Leben in Fülle.

BILLIONAIRE
HUMAN

BILLIONAIRE HUMAN

IS

WORLDS #1
WEALTH AND BUSINESS BOOK
WITH THE GOLOL TOOLS

HOW TO FEEL, NEED AND
EXPRESS YOUR SUCCESS.

DR. SP ROSENBERG

WHEN IT COMES 2U 🌻🐝

Who wants to read Millionaire Human?

Indeed, this is world´s #1 wealth and business book for Entrepreneurs and Business people. So what about those of you who are told not to be an Entrepreneur or those not having a business? Why should you read this book?

BECAUSE 24 HOURS; SEVEN DAYS A WEEK EVERYTHING HUMANS DO IS GETTING THEIR NEEDS MET: ALL HUMAN BEHAVIOR HAS AN UNMET NEED AT ITS ROOT. WHICH MEANS WE ARE ALL ENTREPRENEURS: THIS BOOK IS FOR YOU BECAUSE YOU SERVE LIFE: YOU DELIVER CONTENT EVERY DAY. LIVING IS DOING BUSINESS.

THIS BOOK DOES NOT STEAL YOUR TIME.

THIS IS THE ONLY BOOK IN THE WORLD WHICH ACTUALLY SAFES YOU MONEY AND TIME, WHICH INCREASE$ YOUR NET WORTH AND CONTRIBUTES TO THE ENRICHMENT OF YOUR LIFE.

GO LOL

(Go Language of Life)

Simon Rosenberg created the Go LoL Communication in order to promote a Business Language that serves Life and contributes to the massive enrichment of Life.

Never before in the history of mankind has someone done a business partnering that comes from the heart and connects with (un)met needs. The GoLoL Business Books is a tool for everyone willing to save immense amounts of CASH, explode their NETWORTH and communicate as a GIGA SPEAKER from the heart and solve EVERY problem that comes up. With Go LoL you reach a clearness and deepness in your negotiation skills as an Entrepreneur that you have literally deal after the deal coming in. With Go LoL People understand that you really care about what they have to say. You give them the empathy they need to move on and live the best version of themselves, their business and their entire life.

Speaking like a Millionaire Human is something intensively re-life-ing and something impressively powerful. With Go LoL you do not have to come up with tricks on how to get people's money - they throw money at you because they see how much you are willing to make their life more beautiful and that you were the world´s #1 person ever giving them what they needed for such a thirsty long period of time. 99% of people NEED EMPATHY and 99% of people DO NOT KNOW HOW TO ASK FOR IT.

GoLoL can be applied not only in your business relations but also in any situation you are willing to leave the situation to the full satisfaction of everyone involved.

Apply the GoLoL Tools, use Simon Rosenberg´s Network, speak his language, and manifest your SUCCESS at an insane LOW PRICE.

Simon Rosenberg

Lochau 31.08.2019

WHO IS SIMON ROSENBERG?

SP Rosenberg is World´s #1 Wealth and Business Partner with the Go LoL Tools, Serial Entrepreneur, Real Estate Investor and Book Author. He has Businesses on all seven continents and has done more deals in Real Estate than anyone else with the Go LoL Tools. He is a successful Go LoL Coach and made a fortune with the Go LoL Tools in his exclusive coaching sessions world wide. SP has his own Reality Show - From Go LoL to Riches - and since 2019 he also has a radio show in which he shares content based on the Go LoL tools. Recently he has also started with GoLoLFLIX - a monthly subscription based podcast and video platform - for those people who actually want to make money and save time instead of losing time and money while listening to audios or watching videos.

SP is on world stages with JT Foxx in order to coach and adapt people's communication skills to the Millionaire Human Style. Together they form the world's #1 and most successful wealth and business partnering ever done in the history of mankind.

In November 2019 at the world's biggest and most prestigious wealth and business networking event MEGASUCCESS in Los Angeles, Califonnia JT introduced SP Rosenberg as JT Foxx Junior and letting everyone know that SP takes his spot.

He backs shoulders with some of world's most famous entrepreneurs, Sport icons, Politicians and many others and has been featured in some of world's most exclusive magazines and newspapers.

FOREWORD

"Never do anything in life that is not play."
Papa Rosenberg

When I started with Coaching and Go LoL Business Partnering back in 2015 I realized that the power of a communication from the heart is not only a celebration of life but is in fact something that makes me happy from the heart. I always remember how my dad marked my understanding of business and entrepreneurship with his vision that everything in life is play. Some of you now might rebell and tell me that I am a clown and that a serious man does not make such a statement. In fact, I do agree if I look at it from a life-alienated perspective. What I mean here is that if you are living the life you want and if you are creative in order to get your needs met and contribute to the enrichment of life for yourself and others, everything you do is play. Wealth and Business should not be a burden. It is a mutual giving from the heart. A mutual willingness to grow and expand together.

All of you have that natural sense of play, all of you are entrepreneurs, all of you are Millionaire Humans. My vision with this book is to continue and enlighten your life and your business because once a Millionaire Human you are a CommunicationProject Ambassador and the more people join the Project, the easier it is for me to leave this world one day with a smile because then I know that my efforts for a global wellbeing have not been in vain.

Sincerely yours,

Simon Rosenberg

HOW PEOPLE MAKE SIMON ROSENBERG´S LIFE MORE BEAUTIFUL WITH THEIR POWERFUL MESSAGE

"He takes my spot."

JT Foxx, World´s #1 Wealth and Business Coach

"Simon is a serial entrepreneur and my connection with this individual goes far from business. This man is the kind of friend you find spontaneously and make a strong bond right away as his heart says trust."

"I am really good at observing people and this one is indeed from his heart. With the legacy his father left, now he is eagerly creating good around the world. If you are this person who likes freshness and kind hearted people definitely you will start to be his follower. His message is important to the world because knowing the needs of people are essential to understand their motivations."

But, for somebody to know what their needs are and speak up, you have to learn to connect honestly with yourself and others. Not everybody has this naturally, so here he comes showing you to discover this in his practical ways with a big touch of compassion.

I am glad to fly around the world with Simon and connect with Entrepreneurs, so that they learn to apply the power of the Go LoL Tools in their businesses.

With Millionaire Human Simon gives Entrepreneurs insights into the World of how you are able to turn your business into a Millionaire Business by speaking from the heart with the Go LoL Tools."

Annelise Palacias, CEO of CommunicationProject

"I have read more business books than I can even begin to remember. I have attended numerous conferences and summits. I have heard coaches, experts, and gurus of all kinds. Some really know their value and others just proclaim they do. Bit all too often, it becomes evident that many of them are, more than anything, " Iconic in their own minds."

"Simon Rosenberg is the real deal. He is an expert on Language Of Life. He breaths and lives by it and he is the true example of his teachings."

"After listening to him for the first time at the conference coffee break, I realised that he is the expert that really teaches what he knows, not what he thinks he knows."

"When Simon asked me to write the foreword for this book and sent me the manuscript, I knew even without finishing the script that this is a very rare book indeed."

"There are very few people who have mastered the business skills of really listening what people need, and there are fewer still who have mastered these skills and can explain what works in simple enough terms to ensure that their readers get it."

Simon is one of those rare author-experts.

"The Human Millionaire is exactly what the title claims to be. It will teach you how to turn your expertise into your fortune, and it could potentially make you a very wealthy person. You determine what wealth means to you!"

"If you want to learn how to turn your knowledge into financial freedom, this book may be your best chance to live your dream."

"The purpose of learning is not "Knowing", as most people think it is, but the purpose of learning is "Mastery."

"One of the reasons Simon is so successful - and has been able to help so many others become successful - is that he focuses on mastery *first. Then, he stacks the skills that he has mastered to help other people produce an exponential results!"*

"So if you want to have a quantum leap in your business growth, then you are holding in your hands the key to growing your wealth fast."

"If you will follow Simon's advice in this book, obviously you need to have a pen and paper handy to take action on it immediately, it could cut years off of your learning curve!"

"I want to end this foreword by doing three things. First of all, I want to thank Simon Rosenberg for writing it! Secondly, I want to congratulate you for taking the time to read it! The last thing I want to do in the foreword is to challenge you to put it all into practice. When you do that, you will be able to Change your life and the ones you touch."

Ragne Sinikas, Founder of World Women Conference and Awards, How to Dominate your Decade Talk Show and Starpreneurs TV

THANK YOU WITH GO LOL

IS A MANIFESTATION OF GRATITUDE FROM THE HEART AND A CELEBRATION OF LIFE.

Thank you

To my mum Angelika. For her love and her life-long willingness to support me and taking care of my needs as a human being.

Thank you

To my beloved dad, who showed me the path of life with a language that makes me happy from the heart whenever I connect with the powerful energy that I find communication that serves everyone's needs.

Thank you

To my coaches, who support and coach me and constantly show me my limitations and support me on my learning process in this world, so that I am able to learn from my limitations.

Thank you

To my friend and LoL Mentor Alex, for his inspiration and his interest. Alex gave me the empathy I needed to stop talking and get my vision done.

The sunflower with the bees became the symbols of the Go LoL Brand and whenever I see it, I am connected with the love, the empathy and the compassion I need in this world. My dad is the sunflower, I am the bee.

TABLE OF CONTENTS

The Go LoL Tools 19

CardioWorkout 22

Feelings and Needs List 25

Chapter 1: Disconnected from Life equals unrealistic Dreams 29

CardioWorkout Exercise 1: What is a Millionaire Heartset? 31

Chapter 2: Millionaire Time Management with the Go LoL Tools ... 33

CardioWorkout Exercise 2: Millionaire Human Quiz 36

Chapter 3: Go LoL Business - Everyone wins 45

CardioWorkout Exercise 3: How to approach a Millionaire? 47

Chapter 4: Go LoL Business versus Life-alienated Business 51

CardioWorkout Exercise 4: Branding Ideas with GoLoL Tools 53

Chapter 5: How to become a Millionaire Human yourself 57

CardioWorkout Exercise 5: Is that a Go LoL Business Deal? 59

Chapter 6: Go LoL Marketing Strategies 63

CardioWorkout Exercise 6: The 30 WorkOut Plan 65

Chapter 7: Branding with Go LoL Tools 67

CardioWorkout Exercise 7: Successful Go LoL Businesses 69

Chapter 8: Start connecting and get your Vision done 73

CardioWorkout Exercise 8: Go LoL Entrepreneur "Stress Test" 74

Go LoL Bonus 77

Feelings and Needs Agreement 78

GoLoLFlix.com 79

Connect with Simon Rosenberg 80

THE GO LOL TOOLS

*"What I want in my Life is compassion,
a mutual giving from the Heart."*

SP Rosenberg

Go LoL

ObserverTank
NeedsTank
WishTank

The Go LoL Tools enable you to establish life-serving relations with whoever you are speaking with. Once you decide to apply this three step process your communication is already guaranteed to have the complete satisfaction you wish to obtain for yourself and the person, the group you are talking with.

In the ObserverTank you observe the facts. Would you like to observe with your heart? Millionaire Humans observe with their heart, because the more you are able to connect with other people's needs, the more people are willing to take care of your business. Your net worth depends on your ability to observe without telling other people what you think. When people realize that you do not want to change them or their behaviour, they connect with your bank account. However, a real Millionaire Human and a real Go LoL Entrepreneur asks for more than just Cashflow. In a Go LoL Business Relation you wish for a flow between yourself and your Business Partners based on a mutual giving fomr the heart. Once you are able observe with the heart you are able to see, hear, smell, feel, taste - experience - the common humanity.

Objective observations require zero-based thinking. What you think might destroy your business. Make one ill-considered remark - disconnect from life - and to LOSE the big deals for your business. Once your reputation is ruined, it takes a lot of effort to re-establish the human need for trust in you and your business. Ninety-nine percent of Entrepreneurs and in fact 99% of people are not aware of the fact that Feelings are a result of their (un)met Needs. If you start holding other people accountable for your feelings, NOBODY is ever willing to do business with you again. Observations trigger you a Feeling as a result of a need. And by the way 7 Billion people have the same needs, so do not come up with the excuse that you do not know what another person needs.

In the NeedsTank you are willing to connect with the needs and you are looking for (un)met needs you face in your communication. Time and again, the more effective you communicate, the more you are able to fulfill everyone's needs, the bigger the gratitude people experience. And once people and business partners get the empathy they need, they are able to move on to the transaction. So again, your success equals your ability to connect with human nature.

In today's market economy you cannot take the risk of communicating life-alienated.

Finally, in the WishTank it is the step, in which it comes to the mutual agreement. You as the Go LoL Entrepreneur, you only want another person to fulfill your wish, if this does not disconnect the other person from Life. If the other person's needs are not met, they are not supporting you based on a mutual giving from the heart. These kind of relations destroy your business. Look at the history of mankind. Do you want history to repeat itself? It is your communication that shapes this world. So if you really are a Millionaire Human, communicate with a Language that serves needs. I want to leave this world with the certainty that my life had an impact and made life more beautiful for myself, others and those who come after me. What do you want for your Life?

By the way, a NO is an invitation to start the three step process again. A NO indicates to you that there are still needs that are waiting to be fulfilled. Don't be afraid of a difficult message. I am gonna hold your hand on your learning process. 7 Billion people know the Go LoL Tools but 99% of people are not aware of how to use them. I am doing all this for you to show you how you can communicate the best version of yourself - the millionaire human version of yourself.

CARDIO WORKOUT

Life - Enriching

" Once a famous man promoted "Mens sana in corpore sano!", which now reads - in the Go LoL Tools Entrepreneurs World - "Healthy Heart for a healthy Business".

SP Rosenberg ft. Juvenal

Whoever is willing to speak from the heart, whoever is willing to succeed like a Millionaire Human, whoever is willing to take his/her communication to the next level, whoever is willing to be a serial Go LoL Entrepreneur, whoever is willing to contribute to the enrichment of life, is definitely asking for exercises. Exercises which come from the Heat and increase the net worth. Are there any such tools available.. Not yet. Therefore you are extremely lucky to have this book because nowhere else do you find CardioWorkout exercise which protects your heart, makes your heart stronger and leaves you more MONEY in your pocket. Your Wealth is a function of your cardiac output. Cardiac output is a term often used in medical stress testing for athletes, it is also a valid diagnostic tool to measure heart functionality. Millionaire Humans use the Term Cardiac Output in order to increase their communication rate which is not based on intellectual understanding, but rather as an indicator of how much work remains for them to really speak, communicate and do business from the heart in an absolutely heart-alienated environment. Always remember it takes only one person to apply the Go LoL Tools and you are going to change your business forever. Once you give your heart the exercises, your success and eventually your net worth curve can not go anywhere else than to the highest peak of your success and you reach goal after goal adding more and more value to you and your business. Start now and make the best decision you have ever made in your life. The more you give your heart stage time in your life, more beautiful your life becomes, greater the deals you do become, more people connect with your bank account and more businesses you own. I can tell you, that I would be way more in advance with all my businesses if I had only started earlier with CardioWorkouts. I hope that you will get this massive benefit from the CardioWorkouts I am going to propose you in this book. Let's get it done together. Let's increase your health together. A healthy business requires a healthy heart. The more you exercise, the more you repeat the Go LoL Tools during a 24H day period, the more you are going to where you actually belong. Listen to your heart as often as you are willing to do so and success will come. I guarantee you that If you are 100% sure that with the right communication tools you are going to explode with your business , you are on the way to join the Hall of Fame. If you start little - let´s say one CardioWorkout a Day - and you increase constantly - who will ever be able to stop you ? Nobody except your mind. So turn off the voices in your mind telling you that you will never make it, that success is not for you or that communication from the heart does not work. Start living and your heart will raise you up to more than you have ever imagined in your life.

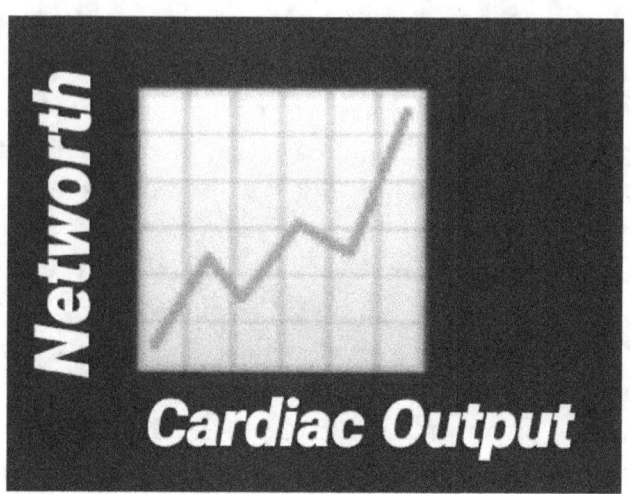

FEELINGS AND NEEDS LIST

FEELINGS

How we are likely to feel when we reach our Millionaire Human level?

Fulfilled, Absorbed, Buoyant, Interested, Alert, Spellbound, Expectant, Alive, Invigorated, Amused, Optimistic, Ardent, Aroused, Relieved, Joyful, Astonished, Blissful, Sensitive, Breathless, Calm, Exhilarated, Refreshed, Carefree, Overwhelmed, Cheerful, Comfortable, Touched, Complacent, Trusting, Composed, Perky, Expectant, Contented, Surprised, Curious, Dazzled, Delighted, Eager, Ebullient, Wide-awake, Effervescent, Elated, Pleased, Enchanted, Relaxed, Encouraged, Trusting, Engrossed, Involved, Exultant, Free, Glad, Glorious, Animated, Glowing, Thrilled, Gratified, Happy, Appreciative, Hopeful, Inquisitive, Confident, Inspired, Fascinated, Intrigued, Trusting, Invigorated, Joyous, Loving, Jubilant, Keyed-up, Mellow, Intense, Mirthful, Tranquil, Moved, Optimistic, Gleeful, Overjoyed, Peaceful, Ecstatic, Pleasant, Proud, Expansive, Quiet, Radiant, Concerned, Rapturous, Enthusiastic, Refreshed, Satisfied, Amazed, Secure, Enlivened, Serene, Splendid, Affectionate, Stimulated, Tender, Cool, Energetic, Thankful, Excited, Friendly, Upbeat, Warm, Grateful, Helpful, Adventurous, Merry.

How we are likely to feel when we apply the bankruptcy slang?

Dull, Afraid, Listless, Aggravated, Jealous, Aloof, Frustrated, Anguished, Forlorn, Annoyed, Frightened, Scared, Anxious, Downcast, Apathetic, Repelled, Aroused, Concerned, Ashamed, Beat, Terrified, Bewildered, Blah, Blue, Bored, Unconcerned, Broken-hearted, Chagrined, Pessimistic, Cold, Hurt, Cross, Dejected, Shaky, Depressed, Sorry, Despairing, Gloomy, Despondent, Horrified, Disappointed, Alarmed,

Discouraged, Unhappy, Disenchanted, Miserable, Indifferent, Disgusted, Unnerved, Dismayed, Nervous, Distressed, Woeful, Disturbed, Downhearted, Edgy, Exhausted, Fatigued, Tired, Fidgety, Unsteady, Furious, Guilty, Harried, Hostile, Hot, Detached, Humdrum, Impatient, Helpless, Intense, Irate, Embarrassed, Irked, Irritated, Jittery, Keyed-Up, Lazy, Leery, Lonely, Mad, Displeased, Mean, Fearful, Morose, Apprehensive, Mournful, Nettled, Disgruntled, Numb, Overwhelmed, Panicky, Aggravated, Passive, Puzzled, Rancorous, Reluctant, Angry, Resentful, Sad, Confused, Sensitive, Hesitant, Skeptical, Disheartened, Sleepy, Lethargic, Sorrowful, Disquieted, Spiritless, Exasperated, Surprised, Tepid, Listless, Troubled, Uncomfortable, Uneasy, Perplexed, Unglued, Bitter, Upset, Startled, Uptight, Vexed, Weary, Horrible, Wistful, Confused, Withdrawn, Heavy, Worried, Agitated, Wretched, Suspicious, Restless, Mopey, Disaffected, Embittered, Shocked.

NEEDS

Millionaire Humans are aware that human nature is the same on all seven continents and that only a communication based on human needs will lead to ways that eventually everyone's needs are fulfilled.

- Give and receive acceptance
- Choosing visions, goals and wishes and plans to get visinos, goals and wishes fulfilled
- Spending life time for a life-serving purpose
- Celebrating Life, business deals and visions fulfilled
- Celebrating losses: loved ones, opportunities
- Authenticity
- Creativity
- Self-worth

- Receiving gratitude for a contribution to get other people's needs met
- Closeness and connection with other human beings
- Being with other human beings
- Exposure
- Contribution to the enrichment of life
- Emotional safety for everything that is alive
- Empathy - someone who is fully with another person but not full of the other person
- Food and Beverage
- Exercising
- Protection from life-threatening forms of life and life-alienated communication
- Regeneration
- Honesty that enables us to learn from our limitations as human beings
- Love - expressed as a mutual giving from the heart
- Reassurance in stormy moments
- Respect for one's uniqueness
- Support in moments of struggle
- Safety to choose plans that lead to the complete satisfaction of goals, visions and wishes in life
- Trust in the loving and compassionate nature every person has
- Understanding from the heart for what a human being needs
- Sexual Expression

- Education that enables to continuously learn and acquire new competences

- Sleep

- Real estate or other forms of shelter

- Touch - as an expression of how much another person cares about you

- Humor which makes life more beautiful

- Beauty and Magnificence

- Harmony with yourself and others

- Inspiration in order to advance as a human being

- Order in life

- Peace - internal and external

CHAPTER 1

DISCONNECTED FROM LIFE EQUALS UNREALISTIC VISIONS

"If you keep doing the same things over and over again and expect a different result, that is called insanity."

JT Foxx

After years of coaching and with my family's tradition to coach other people, I am now giving you some insights why disconnecting from life is not only a risky move for your business but also a life-threatening decision you take for yourself personally.

If you run around with the belief that the "good" deserves reward and the "bad" deserves punishment, you are doing the same things over and over again. You repeat the principle that has done too much harm to businesses all around the world and brought misery in this world from century to century. Do you want to throw this communication away and become a Millionaire Human now?

Well, the stage is yours. You have the tools to impact this world with your communication. Connect with your needs, give empathy and see how your efforts pay out for your business and make life more beautiful for yourself and others.

The massive success you face as a Millionaire Human reflects your communication skills. If you make people see the common humanity, they engage in cooperative relations and want to contribute to a greater picture of success because empathy initiates the mutual giving from the heart.

CARDIO WORKOUT

EXERCISE 1

WHAT IS A MILLIONAIRE HEARTSET?

*"On ne voit bien qu'avec le coeur,
l'essentiel est invisible pour les yeux."*

Le petit prince by **Antoine de Saint Exupér**

"You can be the smartest person in the world but if people don't like you, they will not do business with you."

JT Foxx

From left to right: Bruny Surin, Steven Bradbury, SP Rosenberg, Stedman Graham, and JT Foxx.

A lot of people ask me about the Millionaire Heartset and want me to describe it. They want me to tell them how to reach my level of success.

They urge me to share my secrets with them. And that is precisely what I want to do. I speak at conferences to thousands of people and everywhere I go, I tell people to do a CardioWorkout - because in order to live with a Millionaire HeartSet instead of a Mindset you need a few things to be assured.

- <u>Zero based thinking.</u> You literally need to FORGET EVERYTHING you have been thaught.

- <u>Go LoL Needs List</u> **You need to focus entirely on the needs 7 Billion people have in common.**

And that is it. Now, some of you might stand up and say that I am very superficial and that this was very easy. It is, I agree. It is so natural and human that everyone of us can do it. BUT it is soooo difficult because we have been trained not to use our HeartSet.

In the following chapters you have the opportunity to exercise and improve your cardiac output. DON'T miss this opportunity. I know that over 50% of readers will NOT do it. But those of you who will do so, will have massive success in their communication because they are prepared for the one person, the one opportunity that changes your life forever. Living the life of a millionaire human depends on your ability to get other people needs met. Don't be EURO foolish and tell yourself that you do not need to exercise So many people never reach their highest level of success, because they are not willing to connect with other people's needs.

So, stop diagnosing people and start connecting. Your bank account will be most thankful if you TAKE ACTION NOW and exercise your HeartSet. And do not be afraid, I am here with you and I am gonna hold your hand.

Sincerely yours,

Simon Rosenberg

CHAPTER 2

MILLIONAIRE TIME MANAGEMENT WITH THE GO LOL TOOLS

"While you are fooling around, I earn millions."

Unknown

Entrepreneurs all over the world leave millions and billions on the table while speaking at people. The world belongs to those entrepreneurs who understand TOGETHER. As soon as you start educating people and tell them that they did something wrong, you are disconnected from life and the flow between you and them is blocked.

Which basically translates to a lost deal, a lost opportunity and the unpleasant feelings that are alive as a result of the unmet needs to realize your goals and wishes in your life as an entrepreneur. Millionaire Humans do not have the time nor the money to loose a conversation due to their poor communication skills. I want you to be prepared for every negotiation you are going to do. Do you know why so many businesses go down? Because the owners are not aware to create a business that adapts itself to what people really need. People want to belong because 7 Billion people need community and consideration.

As a Millionaire Human with the Go LoL Tools you observe, you connect with your own needs, you give empathy for what your partners are going through and you eventually express a wish towards the person you are communicating with.

What people really want is empathy. I remember how often my dad told me about that. A lot of people want empathy. But honestly, have you ever been trained to ask someone for empathy? I wish I had listened to that wise and well-considered advice. I would have made a lot more money knowing that. However, what makes me look with the Eye of a Millionaire in the Future is the fact that I am now aware of the Power the Go LoL tools hold for myself and the many businesses I am involved in.

Save your time, save other people's time with a life-enriching communication based on mutual needs. If people feel comfortable in your company, they will take care of your company because again you initiated the mutual giving in them. This is called "motivation-based learning". People see and experience the well-being you create with your communication and they will follow you out of their own motivation to be a Millionaire Human.

A lot of coaches tell people how to be more efficient with their time management. I met so many entrepreneurs who show me their time templates and as I am not impressed by it, I often earn a blank stare. People wonder how I manage my time so efficiently. I am sharing now my secrets with you. I live the Millionaire Human life. - I am constantly doing, what I need. If my stuff prepares my time schedule and it does not allow me to get my needs met, then I rather skip meetings, I rather be late, I rather surprise people with my authenticity. I remember once at a very exclusive lunch event in LA with high class business people from all over the world, I was hungry - my need for food was alive in that moment - and so I started serving myself at the buffet while two gentlemen were having a speech and invited us to investment opportunities. I never care about what other people say or think about me and in the end I closed a multi-millionaire deal with one of the attendees because she actually thanked me for my honesty and authenticity. We closed the deal on the restaurant table - surrounded by lots of empty plates.

What is the take home message here? Millionaire Humans value their needs. Because If YOU DO NOT VALUE YOUR NEEDS; IF YOU DO NOT RESPECT THEM AND GIVE THEM THE ATTENTION THEY DESERVE; NOBODY - I repeat this for you Ladies and Gentlemen - NOBODY ELSE WILL DO SO FOR YOU. You have to pay the price. If people see that you are not taking care of yourself, how than will you be able to take care of a business? Do you understand now the importance of this book? This books actually teaches you for 25EUR how to make you behave with an authenticity people want to connect with. People don't care how smart you are, how much money you own - if they do not like you, they will not do business with you. The more you bring life into your schedule, the more needs you are actually able to connect with and remember that fulfilled needs are the safest and most profitable investments. There is always an immediate return rate and I swear to you, that poeple throw their money at you.

CARDIO WORKOUT

EXERCISE 2

MILLIONAIRE HUMAN QUIZ

As an entrepreneur you don't have time to guess. If you need time to think about it, you loose the deal. If you are not able to answer any questions right away, people search for someone else who can. You can be the smartest person in the world, you can have the greatest fortune of all time, who cares? If you are not able to hear the needs in a message, you are 100% sure to die out as a business. Do you want that?

Yes.

No.

I suppose you scream from the bottom of your heart noooo because otherwise you would not continue with this book. I am very happy that you are still with me and I therefore gift you this Millionaire Human Quiz. I am actually the first man on this planet who offers you a quiz, in which you always win. In which you increase your NET WORTH, the only quiz in the world which makes you CASH immediately - sent right away to your bank on your name in the same minute you are doing this.

CAREFUL this means that you are going to make money in the next 5 minutes. Have you ever had a book like that in your hands before? I wish I had when I was not a Millionaire Human.

What is Money?

- ☐ A need.
- ☐ Life.
- ☐ Energy.
- ☐ Payment.
- ☐ An opportunity to make life more beautiful.

What is Capitalism?

- ☐ Fake.
- ☐ Life-Alienated.
- ☐ Business as usual.
- ☐ An Opportunity to make money.
- ☐ A system that serves basic human needs.

What ia a Business Plan?

- ☐ Plan to get needs met.
- ☐ Fake.
- ☐ Just a sheet.
- ☐ Necessary.
- ☐ Old paradigm.

What is a Marketing Strategy?

- ☐ An opportunity to make life more beautiful.
- ☐ An opportunity to serve the market.

☐ An opportunity to survive as a business.

☐ An opportunity to lose a lot of money.

☐ An opportunity to get more people´s needs met.

Who is a competitor?

☐ A target.

☐ A role-model.

☐ An enemy.

☐ A human being.

☐ A honesty to learn from one´s limitations.

What is a Trade Law?

☐ A barrier for my success..

☐ An obligation in this world.

☐ A limitation for my business.

☐ An invitation to enrich other people's lives. .

☐ A violation of my freedom.

What about taxes and fees?

☐ A necessary evil.

☐ A punishment for every business owner.

☐ An Invitation to make life more beautiful.

☐ A contribution to the wellbeing of others.

☐ A "must-do" thing.

What is a loan?

- ☐ An enrichment of life.
- ☐ A burden for your business.
- ☐ A sign of weakness.
- ☐ A celebration of life.
- ☐ A plant to serve life.

What is an investment?

- ☐ Money 4 Money Exchange.
- ☐ A "you work -I earn" Deal.
- ☐ A manifestation of life.
- ☐ An energy input.
- ☐ An opportunity to make life more beautiful for everyone.

What is Business Partnering?

- ☐ A business relation.
- ☐ Sort of a relationship.
- ☐ A mutual giving from the heart.
- ☐ Two people, one need.
- ☐ A contribution to the wellbeing of others.
- ☐ Mutual giving from the heart.

What about advertising and attention gathering?

- ☐ Wasting money.
- ☐ Not necessary for my business.
- ☐ I do not know about it.
- ☐ First step in order to increase conversion rate.
- ☐ A plan to spread the message of hope.

What is an Employee?

- ☐ A cost factor.
- ☐ A necessary evil.
- ☐ An enemy.
- ☐ A replaceable work-force.
- ☐ A contributor to my wellbeing.
- ☐ An entrepreneur.
- ☐ A Go LoL Business Partner.

What is a salary?

- ☐ An exchange Money-Versus-Time.
- ☐ An investment.
- ☐ A return.
- ☐ An old fashion habit from ancient times.
- ☐ A contribution to another person's wellbeing.
- ☐ Saying thank-you without words.

What is a NDA?

- ☐ A life-guard in today's market economy.
- ☐ A protection of my rights.
- ☐ A mutual agreement.
- ☐ A life-alienated document.
- ☐ A willingness to fulfill everyone's needs.

Which businesses need contracts?

- ☐ Every Business.
- ☐ High level Businesses.
- ☐ Multi-Million Dollar Companies.
- ☐ Small Fishes.
- ☐ Go LoL Businesses.

What is an Entrepreneur?

- ☐ A creator.
- ☐ A fool.
- ☐ A coach.
- ☐ A role-model.
- ☐ A tragic figure.
- ☐ A greedy person.

What is a Bank?

- ☐ An opportunity to get needs met.
- ☐ An enemy of small and medium sized businesses.
- ☐ A nightmare.
- ☐ A pathway to the ultimate enrichment of life.
- ☐ It's only about money.

What is THE investor secret?

- ☐ Invest when others invest.
- ☐ Invest with others.
- ☐ Invest in life-.enriching business.
- ☐ Invest with human nature.
- ☐ Invest in human needs.

What about Charity?

- ☐ For good people.
- ☐ For generous people.
- ☐ An "I-give-you-take" mentality.
- ☐ A moral obligation.
- ☐ A fake news thing..
- ☐ A contribution to the wellbeing of others.
- ☐ A Business.
- ☐ An opportunity to disconnect from human needs.

| Who is the next Millionaire Human? |

- ☐ SP Rosenberg.
- ☐ You.
- ☐ Everyone on this planet.
- ☐ The top 1% of world's population.
- ☐ Readers of this book.
- ☐ Successful people.
- ☐ Life connected people.

After having completed the entire quiz, you can send your answers to simon.rosenberg@da-vienna.at . This is my private EMail and I guarantee you, that I ANSWER EVERY EMAIL myself.

Everyone who sends in the answers is automatically registered for the annual christmas lottery which offers an ULTIMATE, TOP VIP AND ABSOLUTELY EXCLUSIVE experience with Simon Rosenberg.

CHAPTER 3

GO LOL BUSINESS - EVERYONE WINS

"I love the fact that you promote the abundance-based approach in Business."

Jim Alvino

When I started Go LoL Business people would turn their head and say that it will never work out well. That people will abuse my approach for their own profits.

Well, I can tell you that figures don't lie. I could mention so many stories in which I as World´s #1 Wealth and Business Partner with the Go LoL Tools have been in exactly those situations where I saw the power of a mutual giving from the heart and how people took care of me without me ever asking them for anything.

Successful businesses are those, who are life-connected and aware of a communication that serves life. I want you to be aware that people might be sceptical at the beginning. DO NOT EDUCATE THEM. They have had the bad experience of education TOO MANY TIMES. What people want is that you fulfill their need for authenticity and autonomy and if you are able to do that for them, they make you the winner personality everyone wishes to be. Your success is SOOOOOO close. It is just one word away. How you communicate is how you succeed. Go LoL Business DOES NOT MEAN that you have to change a whole system - that has by the way helped so many people to a life-style we take nowadays for a very normal normality - what you do is communicate with the Go LoL Tools. Remember: First the ObserverTank, second the NeedsTank and you finish the Millionaire Human Communication Style with the WishTank. Networth? Everyone wins.

Earning your worth has never been easier. Connect with your needs, connect with other people's needs and you grow and explode TOGETHER.

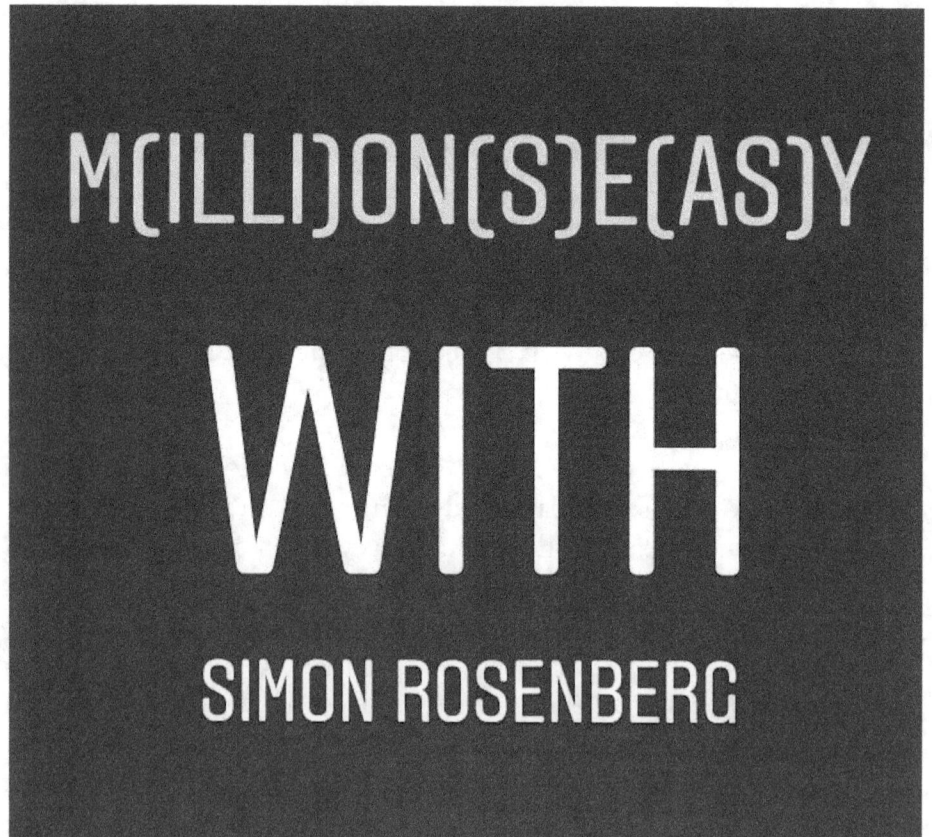

CARDIO WORKOUT

EXERCISE 3

HOW TO APPROACH A MILLIONAIRE?

One of the reasons why so many people are actually afraid of going to the next level of their success is the result of a life-alienated education that taught them whether something was right or wrong instead of showing them what they really need in life.

The effect of such an education is that millions communicate life-alienated and only the top 1% of people communicate in ways that make them reach the best version of themselves, earning their worth and living the life they want. Your success is just a few words away. Think about it. One world could change your life forever. Do you want to miss such an opportunity? Do you want your communication to stand between you and your ultimate success?

If the answer is no, I am willing to share with you a few aspects here on how to approach a millionaire. It also works for billionaires. So you actually get two pieces of information which gonna change your life for the price of one. Do you see how much I am willing to contribute to the enrichment of your life?

Empathy.	If you are unable to empathize with those people who are more successful than you, you will never make it to the next level.
Time.	If you don't have time for your success why should anyone take care of your ideas? They do not need your ideas, they are already part of the Top 1% of the world's population.

Authenticity.	How can you ever expect someone to connect with your needs if you are not aware of your own needs? What people appreciate most is authenticity. If you give them the impression, that you are not true to your own needs, you block the flow between them and you.
Persistence.	One of my ultimate success secrets is my continued willingness to advance my ideas. There is a difference between stalking and persistency. Persistence with the Go LoL Tools reflects your willingness to propose deals and opportunities at the right moment when a business partner is able to say yes.
Heart-only reasoning.	A lot of people believe that the heart is not the #1 organ for decision making. I can tell you that I made my millions in exactly those moments in which I have listened to my heart. And I wish I had done that more often. I would be way more advanced. Whenever you give attention to your heart, you are 100% connected with life and you do not have to fear anything because a decision from the heart is a Millionaire Human wise.
Zero-based thinking.	If however you continue to analyse, judge, diagnose, evaluate, blame, complain, ... about your observations, you are disconnected from life. And as an immediate result, people will disconnect from your bank account.

CardioWorkout.	Communication from the heart is like a sport. The more you exercise, the better you become. IT IS NOT A QUESTION OF WHETHER YOU ARE TALENTED OR NOT: The Success you achieve with a CardioWorkout is a linear function of time. The more time you apply the Go LoL Tools, the more often you communicate like a Millionaire Human, THE MORE SUCCESSFUL YOU ARE GONNA BE.
Language of Life.	With a Language of Life, you are always safe. No matter what you do. You are 100% guaranteed to succeed. In any business. In EVERY relation. In your relationships. Once applied, always successful.
Knowledge.	Knowledge based on life-enriching education is always requested. The more you are able to serve other people's needs, the more they will take care of you and your business.
Rapid implementation.	Phrases like "I will think about it", "I have to wait for", "It is not the right time", "Let's wait and see", are expressions that make your partners believe that you are not a stable and reliable person. A Millionaire Human says "Thank you for your information. My need for …. Is not met here. Would you be willing to contribute to my wellbeing with …." Always be very clear about what you need. Be very clear with people about what you need. Give them a clear and understandable definition of what you need for a heart-felt YES.

| Flexibility. | Needs change every second as a result of our ever changing environment. If you are unable to adapt to our ever changing economy, you are 100% sure to die out as a business.

Flexibility with the Go LoL Tools means that you are proficient - as A communicator - in understanding other people's needs. |
|---|---|
| Tolerance | Tolerance requires you to know your own needs first. Only in doing so, you are able to understand what other people need. You learn to see the common humanity and you learn to value the needs all humans share with each other. |
| Honesty | As a millionaire human, honesty is a communication that allows you to learn from your limitations. |
| Trust | A lot of entrepreneurs complain to me in my Go LoL Coachings about people not being loyal to them. That they are not able to trust anyone. I agree. I do not trust anyone who does not speak from the heart. Trust in a Language of Life World implicates ONLY that people tell you how they feel as a direct result of their (un)met needs. |
| Respect. | Respect does not equal anarchy. It means that you are aware of your needs, you value your needs, you see the common humanity in your communication partners and you therefore hear their needs IT DOES NOT MEAN THAT YOU FULFILL THEIR NEEDS. |
| Community. | People need to belong to something. The more you are able to connect people to your business, to your life as an entrepreneur, the more you met their need for community, the more they are mutually giving from the heart. |

CHAPTER 4

GO LOL BUSINESS VERSUS LIFE-ALIENATED BUSINESS

"Wer zu spät kommt, den bestraft das Leben."
"Life punishes those who come too late."

Michail Gorbatschow

The famous quote by Mr. Gorbatschow perfectly captures the main and core message of the Go LoL approach in business. As an experienced Millionaire Human, I can tell you right away - when I hear people communicate - about their net worth. Your words, your communication shape your personal growth and the growth curve of your business.

With the Go LoL Tools you stay connected in these conversations, you connect with the needs you hear behind the words. You ask back and sometimes you just keep silent and give the empathy people need. Once I had such an experience in a hotel lobby. Due to my remarkable physical appearance a lot of people come to me and want to take pictures. So this gentleman. We started a conversation. He started to scream and shout at my Go LoL Approach. He jumped around me and people were staring at us. However, I managed to keep myself focused on the empathy I wanted to give this gentleman. After two hours he came to me, shook my hand, told me that I was a lovable man, a good soul and that he wants to be my friend and business-partner. It turned out to be one of my best time-investments I ever made.

Be honest with yourself. How many times a day are you connected with your needs? And how many times are you connected with other people's needs? Do you understand now the many lost opportunities to monetize your relations? Businesses go down because Entrepreneurs are trained to communicate life-alienated. Being aware of that communication deficit, you are now able to turn this into your niche. Start connecting with what people want in their life and their business and support others on their way to get rid of a life-alienated approach in Life and in business.

The tragedy of itself repeating financial crises, recessions, stock markets hitting negative records, great depression, real estate bubbles. Inflation, fort closer, bankruptcy … are just a few examples of how life-alienated communication, my dad used to call it "Amtssprache", negatively affects business. No business man is immune to such a language. You can be the greatest Go LoL Entrepreneur but if you live in a life-alienated world, you are also exposed to the dangers of such a communication. What can you do? Connect with those people you care about your needs. Be as creative as possible to get your needs met.

I give you a personal example here. During the Corona Virus Hype in Europe in Spring 2020, I made a fortune with Real Estate deals. Despite the accumulating wealth, I did not feel safe nor did I feel happy. Rather I was going through the feelings I mentioned here in the book which are alive when needs are not met. What happened? My need for freedom, my need for choosing my own plans to get my vision done was not met. With closed borders and travel restrictions to the USA, I saw that the limitations negatively affected my wellbeing. Within a day I made the decision to leave Europe behind. I started to invest in foregin markets and I therefore turned a limitation into my biggest strength. Acting fearless and without rethinking it was once my biggest weakness but within hours I turned it into my biggest success secret. I just did what my heart told me to do - GET MY NEEDS DONE. Again, I share this with you, because I want you to be successful as well.

CARDIO WORKOUT

EXERCISE 4

BRANDING IDEAS WITH GOLOL TOOLS

Turning your weaknesses into your biggest strengths, that is my top priority. My Dad was an amazing person. The person I am today is a result of his excellent life-enriching education. The way he brought me up made me a Go LoL Entrepreneur. Whenever I seek advice and guidance, I connect with his powerful messages. He left me so much. From time to time I wish he was still here with me.

Anyway, despite his greatness, he also had his limitations. Unfortunately, he never really worked on them. What he needed was a marketing and branding expert. A gentleman like Apple co-founder Steve Jobs. As we all know, Steve Jobs is no longer among us.

I was looking for a person who could be my Steve Jobs. And it was back in 2019, a foggy day in Austria's capital, Vienna, in a crowded Hilton Hotel conference room, that I met with JT Foxx. JT Foxx is World´s #1 Wealth and Business Coach, Serial Entrepreneur, involved in over 50 businesses all over the world, Real Estate Investor and best-selling author with the Millionaire Underdog book.

Steve Wozniack, Apple Co-founder and long-term friend of Steve Jobs, says about JT that JT is "the closest thing to Steve I have ever met." I found the person who literally changed my life forever. I have found a marketing and branding expert. JT works with George Ross, Donald Trump's former right hand man, backs shoulders with some of the world´s most successful people, coaches in over 40 countries, is the best paid speaker in the World and my friend. Friendship is by the way the most powerful and valuable gift you can ever find in this world. I remember how I felt an immense gratitude from the heart when I understood the value of his knowledge for the Go LoL Tools. What Go LoL Communication needs is a JT Foxx. And therefore I became JT Foxx Junior in Vienna.

From left to right: Mr. Erik Wilson, Me (alias JT Foxx Junior) and JT Foxx.

Success is a choice. With JT I worked on marketing and branding solutions for my business and he told me that my success was just a matter of time. My net worth went from negative 40,000 to 50,000,000 within three months.

Branding with association is the most powerful tool you could ever wish for. It works for every business. If you get an introduction from a person who is more successful than you, you are pretty much guaranteed to succeed. The Go LoL Business Partnering I do today is a direct result of me partnering with JT. I want to share my success with others.

If you want to take your business to the next level, if you are tired of making other people rich, if you are tired of communicating life-alienated, if you wish for more empathy in your business relations, if you want other people to take care of your business, if you want your bank account to explode, if you want your Net Worth to sky-rocket, if you are willing to do whatever it takes to be successful, If you want to earn your worth, if you said yes to all of these proposals, … connect with world´s #1 Wealth and Business Partnering. JT does the Wealth and Business Coaching, I do the Go LoL Coaching. Together all three of us will throw the box away and manifest the best version of you AND your business.

Go LoL Coaching requires a lot of self-initiatives and YOUR willingness to get things done. I share my invitations with you, you decide whether you like to accept or refuse.

Go to *www.gololflix.com*
Go to *www.millionaireflix.com*
Go to *www.simonrosenberg.online*
Go to *www.jtfoxx.com*
Go to *www.sendusdeals.com*
Go to *www.megasuccess.com*

CHAPTER 5

HOW TO BECOME A MILLIONAIRE HUMAN YOURSELF

"The goal of this is not to change people or their behaviour."

Marshall B. Rosenberg

Please do not worry. We are all Millionaire Humans. There is only you. There is no one else like you. You are unique. Now make your communication aligned with your uniqueness.

This leads then to your success as a Millionaire Human and once aware of your needs you can move on and create the success you want to see happening.

It is not easy to leave behind a habit that was with you for years, for some of you it means decades of life-alienated communication. Yes, it is tragic. I had these moments as well, when I realized that I was existing far beneath my worth. Connect with others and profit from human nature. Compassion and empathy will give you the power to move on and start the Millionaire Human life you definitely want for you as you are reading this book.

One of my coaches, Colin, taught me about the abundance this world has in stock for everyone willing to lay their hands on the wealth that is just one word away. My biggest limitation at that time was my mindset. I was telling myself the "disconnected-from-life" story that success was not for me, that money does not make me happy, wealth was out of reach for myself, that I was obliged to wear a white coat in order to help other people´s wellbeing, … Colin coached me to the next level. I started with Go LoL Coaching after I finished the coaching sessions with him in Atlanta, Georgia and my success grew constantly but not with the pace it grows nowadays. However, this first step was mandatory.

From my experience, a lot of people talk about their vision but they fail to express their needs and therefore they never make the first step necessary to become successful. And as a result, they run after a vision for their entire life without ever getting close to it. Just to give you an example. A start-up business owner told me about this goal to raise 100,000,000 USD. I asked him about his company, his business plan, neither the one nor the latter were existing. How can you ever expect someone to invest with you, if you are not able to get their need for safety and trust met?

You might get this wrong when you read it for the first time but sometimes saying no, letting people do insane things over and over again is the hardest thing to do and with which most entrepreneurs fail. The Contribution to the enrichment of life and the wellbeing of others makes us all very giving personalities. However, your success requires a protective no from time to time. Saying yes all the time does not take people to their ultimate success level. They rather get stuck in their mindset and their self-repeating misery. Rather give them the honesty from the heart they need to learn from their limitations.

CARDIO WORKOUT

EXERCISE 5

IS THAT A GO LOL BUSINESS DEAL?

In today's market economy, I want you to be a rapid implementer and a Go LoL Champion. The more you have to think about something. the more time you need to invest, the less successful you are.

In this exercise I want you to make rapid decisions, YES or NO. Are the deals Go LoL Deals, which fulfill everyone's needs? In case you do not feel comfortable making a choice between the yes or no box, tick the Go LoL timeout box.

Again, I invite you to send me your answers to my private email address *simon.rosenberg@da-vienna.at* and I will answer all your messages in person.

Many of the deals I write here for your CardioWorkout are real deals that I have seen in newspapers, saw them on TV, as small ads on the Internet, as street flyers, as stickers on doors and postboxes, heard them on a radio show, …

Proposed Deal	Yes	No	GoLoL Timeout Box
"Call as much as you need"			
"Take two, pay one"			
"Buy now and get a discount on your next purchase"			

"NOW OR NEVER"			
"Eat AS MUCH AS you can"			
"CASH-Back Guarantee"			
"Cheapest SEX in town"			
"We buy your house"			
"Cancel at any time"			
"For members only"			
"Smoking kills"			

"Lending money has never been so quick"			
"Get your credit card tomorrow"			
"White teeth guaranteed"			
"Find you soulmate"			
"Get your licence"			
"University diploma for 100USD"			
"We want you"			
"FREE consultation"			
"Get rich quick"			

"I am your solution"			
"Take what you need"			

"We pay your bills"			
"CASH IMMEDIATELY"			
"Passport for Investors"			
"First Class passengers are asked to proceed to the gates immediately"			
"Free healthcare for everyone"			
"Get MORE for your money"			

What most authors do here is telling you what is right or wrong. I DO NOT give you a correct answer because what I want in my life is compassion. I want you to choose freely and without any fear of punishment. Punishment is far more than most of us understand from it. In only saying that your answer is wrong I limit your own creativity and I hurt you as much as I hurt myself. Real Millionaire Humans want their partners to be independent and successful because the more you give your partners the opportunity to be creative and innovate freely, the more income they create for them and eventually for yourself.

Always remember that communication is the art of success and money is how you monetize your words.

CHAPTER 6

GO LOL MARKETING STRATEGIES

"You are not a coach. You are a mentor."

Manely Ellamo

Go LoL Marketing means that you serve needs. READ WITH CARE NOW. THIS IS GONNA MAKE YOUR BUSINESS A MULTI-MILLION DOLLAR BUSINESS.

The more your product, your services make life more beautiful for your clients, the more they will take care of your business. It is a self-running circle. You serve life and they connect with your bank account. Go LoL Clients don't want you to go through fire and ruin your health to get cheap products on the market. In a Go LoL Business relation - REMEMBER THAT - people do business because they interact on a mutual giving and receiving from the heart. Go LoL Marketing is therefore a marketing that connects with unmet needs and specifically addresses these needs. Use the feelings of your clients as an indicator for your business. If they feel the feelings listed previously when needs are met, you can be 100% sure that you serve life and that you are already a Go LoL Entrepreneur.

Zero-based thinking in Go LoL Marketing means that you listen to needs and you design your products and services accordingly.

Don't stress yourself with new product ideas. People's needs will guide your business branches. As a Millionaire Human you are an active listener and you serve unmet needs on the market with your products or services.

And Out of nowhere you find your niche and people might wonder why you are so successful. Tell them "I communicate with the Go LoL Tools and my marketing is based on the universal human needs".

Your homework today - check the big success stories out there and see how much these companies, these people are able to meet many needs at once. Expanding your business means that you are able to consider and eventually serve more and more needs.

What most Entrepreneurs are not aware of, is the fact that what works in one place does not automatically work out in another one. You can not expect your client base in Europe to serve as an example for expanding your business to the south-asian market. Of course, people have the same need all over the world. That is your unique Go LoL selling proposition. You need a business that serves human needs. And if you are able to connect with local plans to get these needs met, you are most likely to turn your business into a billion EURO company with such little effort that it can literally be considered playing a joyful game. Remember what I told you previously about what my dad told me " Never do anything in Life that is not play."

CARDIO WORKOUT

EXERCISE 6

THE 30 WORKOUT PLAN

It takes 29 days to change an existing habit and a life-time to build an empire. Please remember that it takes one ill considered remark to destroy it all.

Monday

On Monday I invite you to start the week with the following:

1. Take a piece of paper.
2. Write down the feelings and needs list.
3. Write on another piecce of paper the three Go LoL Steps.
4. Put them in your pocket, record them on your smartphone, make a short video.

<u>REMEMBER THAT IT HAS TO BE AS DISRUPTIVE AS POSSIBLE.</u>

For now this is everything you gotta do. Now take your time and enjoy this first monday in your life with the Go LoL Tools. It is the day on which you decide freely and willingly to adapt your life to the life-enriching nature of mankind. May now come the days of compassionate giving and ever lasting success for you and your business.

Mondays have never been so good. Never again will you experience Monday sleepiness because as a Millionaire Human you are doing business when other people are in need of your products, services or investments.

Tuesday, Wednesday, Thursday, Friday, Saturday and Sunday

Once a Millionaire Human it is most important not to loose your wealth. In order to avoid any losses you are invited to practice EVERY day. Not just once but every day. A Go LoL Training plan requires you to take action at all times. Yes, it can be very hard at times. But most important is to take the feelings and needs list with you, so that you are prepared.

I had a CEO who took the feelings and needs list in business card size with him and whenever he got into a conversation and realized that he was losing the connection he needs to stay compassionate, he took a Go LoL Timeout and checked the feelings and needs list. He became a Go LoL Entrepreneur, tendered his resignation as CEO and now works on his own business. He wrote me a message half a year ago, saying that the Go LoL Tools made him a millionaire human. These are the success stories that make me continue with all my efforts for a life-enriching communication all over the world. I have other family members who decided to disappear and live a decent life without all the energy consuming efforts of really going out there and dealing with life-alienated systems. However, I want your success to come out and if I get one of you on the stage of life with the Go LoL Tools, I am more than happy about the result. And if you, dear reader, decide to spread the feelings and needs language, we can get it done and serve a greater purpose TOGETHER.

The 30 Days CardioWorkout Plan

Implement	Repeat	Repeat	Repeat	Repeat	Repeat	Repeat
Repeat	Repeat	Repeat	Repeat	Repeat	Repeat	Repeat
Repeat	Repeat	Repeat	Repeat	Repeat	Repeat	Repeat
Repeat	Repeat	Repeat	Repeat	Repeat	Repeat	Repeat

CHAPTER 7

BRANDING WITH GO LOL TOOLS

"Be a transformational Entrepreneur."

JT Foxx

Branding with the Go LoL Tools means that you are perfectly aware of needs, that you know what needs you are able to fulfill with your product, your service, your investment opportunity.

As a Millionaire Human you are doing business because you want to contribute to the enrichment of Life. Often people mistake me with this quote. Of course, I do not work for free. Who does? But what you represent with your brand and what your company brand represents is a guarantee for a communication that aims to make this world more beautiful for everyone.

Money is a plan to get needs met and as long as people exchange money to fulfill needs, why should a millionaire human refuse to do so? Remember that Millionaire Humans never want to change people or their behaviours. The Millionaire Mindset with the Go LoL Tools is smart enough and sufficiently connected with life, so that eventually everyone's needs are met - IN THE GIVEN AND ESTABLISHED STRUCTURES:

Despite the fact that Go LoL Entrepreneurs do not have a competitor, you have a rough environment out there. Whether you are a start-up or a "big fish" in an ocean of fake, you need to be 100% sure about what you wish for. Ther clearer you are about it, the more confident you are going to present yourself on the floor. Successful brands are created when people connect the brand with feelings that are alive as a result of fulfilled needs. In today's markets you survive not as a result of how great you are but rather as a direct effect of how well your brand name is perceived among your clients. Take the example of two businesses. The one is the best restaurant owner in town with an excellent reputation and the other one a very average restaurant chief but with a "Steve Jobs" -like branding and marketing mindset. Who is gonna survive? The one with better branding and marketing. Communicating with the Go LoL Tools does not mean that you have to refuse marketing and branding knowledge. But whenever you apply it, make sure that you are aware of you making the choice and that you know the needs which make you opt for such a decision.

If you are able to brand yourself and your result with other successful and life-connected Entrepreneurs, you are definitely a successful Person and you leave this world unforgettable.

CARDIO WORKOUT

EXERCISE 7

SUCCESSFUL BUSINESSES

Here I am about to share some of my successful businesses. This is very exclusive and for Millionaire Human readers only. Enjoy.

GoLoLFLIX

GoLoLFLIX is the netflix for Go LoL Millionaires and Go LoL Billionaires. You find all my coachings, from Geneva to where I am today on GoLoLFLIX. You get daily news updates with a Language of Life. Video and Audio content for your success.

Rosenberg Magazine

The Rosenberg Magazine is the Go LoL Millionaire and Billionaire News Update. You find high quality articles in a Language of Life, weekly reports from all over the world including business, politics, health, real estate, cryptocurrency, travel, interviews and a monthly special on recent Go LoL Success Stories from all around the world.

simonrosenbergapp

The simonrosenbergapp is the World´s #1 Wealth and Business Partnering with the Go LoL Tools App in the world. It is so unique because for the very first time in the history of mankind people get a networking platform specifically designed and created for Go LoL Entrepreneurs. Take a chance now.

Millionaire Human Merchandise

Millionaire Humans have their own style. WIth Millionaire Human Merchandise I offer designers an opportunity to sell their luxury collections with the Go LoL Tools. Probably one of the best businesses I am involved in because I do not have to do anything apart from collecting the deposits at the end of every week.

Go LoL Reality Show

The Go LoL Reality Show is the first ever and follows me in my daily life. I started from negative 40,000 to now accumulated wealth of over 50,000,000 within 3 months.

In the reality show I introduce you to everyday life as a Millionaire Human and you get insight into my meetings, trips, likes and dislikes… Subscription rate is 20EUR a month

Go LoL Mobility

Go LoL Mobility is a collection of luxury cars that enable you to travel around and get your wish for high quality mobility met. You can book a Go LoL Driver and get the coaching while you reach your destination.

Healthenor

The Go LoL Version of a medical doctor is a HealthENOR because MDs who apply a language of life want to connect with what people really need. Therefore, the intention is not only to treat symptoms but rather to connect with the roots of a trigger which limits people's health.

Mr. GoLoL

Mr. GoLoL is the crypto name I use, when I invest in digital currency. Once the Go LoL movement joins a blockchain, the wish to contribute to the enrichment of life runs through cyberspace at the speed of light.

Go LoL Credit Card

The Go LoL Credit Card is a Credit Card which allows its user to spend as much as they need. People who communicate with the Go LoL Tools take what they need and do not want to exploit the margins of the card. Providers and users interact based on a mutual giving from the heart and the two of them simply want to see each others complete satisfaction.

Go LoL SIM card

Community and consideration are important needs human beings share with each other. The Go LoL SIM card is World´s #1 SIM card which allows users to chat, call each other and surf the world wide web based on their need to manifest community. The digital age serves life in all its beauty and magnificence because it enables people to establish an authentic connection with whoever, wherever and whenever.

CHAPTER 8

START CONNECTING AND GET YOUR VISION DONE

Often people connect with me and tell me that they need my help and that they are not able to be successful themselves.

Being successful is lonely at times. People who disconnect from what they really need might attack you and project their misery on you. Some might even blame you for their misery. With the Go LoL Tools you have the communication tools to establish a connection with them but if you take responsibility for their feelings you are only limiting yourself.

Go Language of Life also applies to yourself. The world is big enough and if you are not willing to help someone, do not mind. There are 7,599,999,999 (at the time this book was published) people out there who might be willing to help the one person you are not willing to help. Mutual giving from the heart means that people do not ask something from you, you are not willing to do freely.

Once you decided to follow the path of Life with a Language of Life people will join you because they see how your communication positively affects you. This means that Millionaire Humans are never alone - despite or better DUE TO YOUR SUCCESS.

Sincerely yours,

Simon Rosenberg
World´´s #1 Wealth and Business Partner with the Go LoL Tools.

CARDIO WORKOUT

EXERCISE 8

GO LOL ENTREPRENEUR "STRESS TEST"

Now it is time to show your ability to apply the Go LoL Tools. If you pass the Go LoL Entrepreneur "Stress Test", you will be issued a Certificate, signed by me in person and for 10EUR the certificate will be available as a download on the website *www.millionairehuman.com*

Each matching couple receives 10 points.

What I would likt you to do here, is that you match each word with a Go LoL Translation. The score is calculated based on a Go LoL Score.

Word	Translation	Score
Examples		
Simon	Rosenberg	10/10
Land	England	10/10
Moonlight	Swimming	10/10
Go LoL	Business	10/10
Student	Book	10/10
Luxury	ähm.. ähm	0/10
Holidays	…………..	5/10

Remember that it is always better to say nothing and connect with what you need instead of making an ill-connected remark which is life-alienated and hurts other people. That is why you get 5 out of 10 possible scoring points for a Go LoL Timeout.

Amtssprache		
Violence		
Life		
Charity		
War		
Anger		
Sadness		
Cash		
Networth		
Communication		
Education		
Marketing		
Entrepreneurship		
Millionaire		
Success		
Agriculture		
MD		
CoronaVirus		
Party		
Land		

Crypto		
Real		
Wealth		
Millionaire		

GO LOL BONUS

Go LoL Partnering is a world wide business strategy. There are partners all around the world who are willing to connect with you and partner with you and your business. Together WITH you, they will support you to become a Go LoL Entrepreneur and live exactly the LIFE you want for yourself and others.

Go LoL Partners offer you four specific services:

- Go LoL 🌻 Partnering
- Go LoL 🌻 Speaker
- Go LoL 🌻 Charity
- Go LoL 🌻 Empowerment

Show them your Millionaire Human Book and you receive a 5% discount for the service you ask them for.

THE NDA FOR MILLIONAIRE HUMANS AND GO LOL ENTREPRENEURS

Feelings and Needs Agreement

A Go LoL Agreement is a single page because Go LoL Business Partners co-operate based on a mutual giving from the heart.

I agree that Feelings remind me of my (un)met Needs.

I agree that Needs are the Cause of my Feelings.

I agree that I move on in all my Beauty and Magnificence.

I am willing to contribute to the Enrichment of Life. I am willing to connect with Feelings and Needs.

Signed:

Date :

GOLOLFLIX.COM

GoLoLFLIX is the channel for Go LoL Millionaires. You find Go LoL audios, Go LoL Videos and a platform to connect and do business with everyone willing to do GoLoL Business with you

As you have Millionaire Human right now in your hands when you read this, please be aware that you get access to GoLoLFlIX.com for 19,99EURO monthly. You can cancel your subscription at any time.

MEET SIMON ROSENBERG

If you want to meet Simon Rosenberg, go to his website simonrosenberg.online or meet him at one of his events all around the world.

As a Millionaire Human Book owner Simon Rosenberg gives you access to his inner circle. Exclusive and only for Millionaire Human Book readers, you find here his private E-Mail. Write him, connect with him and live the life you deserve. Write to *simon.rosenberg@da-vienna.at* and you will get Simon Rosenberg´s personal response to anything you ask, tell, request from him

You can also follow Simon Rosenberg on Social Media

Twitter @s_prosenberg

Instagram @s_prosenberg

Facebook @Simon Rosenberg (Personal Page)

Facebook @cplosangels (Go LoL Facebook Page)

Facebook @jtfoxxjunior (Fan Page)

Linkedin Simon Rosenberg

SoundCloud Simon Rosenberg

Youtube Simon Rosenberg

BONUS

World´s #1 Wealth and Business Dictionnary with the Go LoL Tools

For Millionaire Humans only

I give you this Bonus here, because I want you to be successful. I want you to communicate yourself to the next level of your life. I share with you my secrets because what I want in my life is a mutual giving form the heart.

If you use these phrases in your communication you will encounter massive success no matter what you do. No matter who you are talking to. With these phrase you unlock the hidden Millionaire Human inside your heart? You wanna start living and sipt just existing? Well, here you go. These are the tools.

Repeat them 24Hours, 7 days a week. As long as you are still communicating life-alienated there is no time for a recovery phase. All you bring to the table is hard focused work on your communication. These tools make you damn wealthy rich. If you don't use them, nobody cares because you have to pay the price. Do you want to die broke with no money and leave your children your debts because you communicated with Bankruptcy Slang? If not, then you better communicate your a.. off. You are better waking up at 6 am in the morning every day, going to bed at midnight every night

Because as long as you do not communicate the best version of yourself, only hard work and a willingness from the heart will lead you to ultimate MASSIVE success

Nobody has ever done a translation from Millionaire Human communication tools to a bankruptcy slang. So please handle with care and gratitude. I took me a lot of time and I could have use my time way more productive than just simply translating bankruptcy slang in a millionaire and billionaire´s language. But I am doing this, because I am willing to contribute to the enrichment of YOUR life. This list has a networth of exactly 8000EUR. Do you understand now how much I care about your success and how I am adding value to your communication for FREE. This books costs me and my publisher money and time, but when you succeed with your communication, we succeed as well. That is why we are doing this for you.

Millionaire Human	**Bankruptcy Slang**
Would you be willing to…..?	I want you to …
Would you like to ….?	You have to …
What do you need to know from me, so that… .?	You must …
Do you need … to say yes?	You should …
Tell me what you need, I tell you how I feel.	Tell me who your friends are, I tell you who you are.
I have an unmet need.	I need money.
My need is the cause, your action is the trigger.	It's your fault.

Who is able to contribute to my wellbeing?	Help me.
Not aware of my needs.	I am Broke.
I know what I need	I am rich.
What need is alive right now?	How are you doing?

Need-based living.	Strategy-based thinking.
Contribution to the Enrichment of Life.	Investment.

Connected with Life.	Mindfulness.
I take full responsability for my needs because I …	I am angry because you….
I want to serve unmet needs with my products and services.	I want to make money with my business.
I live power WITH my employees because TOGETHER we make things happen.	I have the complete power OVER my employees.
Everything people do is meant to fulfill a human need.	People exploit me.
If I am unable to connect with unmet needs, my business operates life-alienated.	I have to be better than my competitors.
When my needs are not met, I connect with what I really need, what other people need and search for a solution so that eventually all needs are met.	I do as I am told to.
Mutual Agreement.	Compromises.
I appreciate honesty to learn from my limitations.	I know everything.
Needs not met to communicate what I really need.	This is top secret.
I need empathy to give empathy.	Haters want to destroy me.
I am willing to educate life serving.	There are no qualified people out there.

Success is a matter of communication	Success is a matter of choice.
There are people who need a lot of empathy to move on.	Some people will never make it in their life.
First the connection, than the solution.	Make people buy.

If we are unable to make life more beautiful, people search for someone else who makes life more beautiful.	If we don´t increase our sales our company goes down.
Money allows you to get unmet needs fulfilled.	Money does not make you happy.
If I am unable to express my needs, I am not a life-connected Entrepreneur.	Dreams don't come true.
A difficult message is an opportunity to brand my Go LoL Tool based Businesss Model.	A bad reputations hurts my Business.
7.01 (please check the updated number online) people have the same needs.	How am I able to define a perfect target avatar?
99% of people need empathy but do not know how to ask for it.	People will not do business with me because of my background, my appearance, ….
I am at work because I love to contribute to the enrichment of life.	I want vacations and a better salary.
I am willing to give you the value you need.	Can I have a reduction on the Price?
If my request does not contribute to the full satisfaction of another person, I do not want it.	I want things to be for free.
I receive a manifestation of gratitude based on a mutual giving from the heart once I have effectively made another person's life more beautiful.	I exchange time/services/products for money.

Would you be willing to contribute to my wellbeing?	If you do not behave as told to, I punish you.
What is alive when you light a cigarette?	Smoking kills.
This man has a lot of unmet needs.	He is a psychopath.
The words we use limit our compassionate nature.	This world is crazy.
What I want in my life is compassion, a mutual giving from the heart.	Everything is so expensive these days.
More and more people are aware of what they really need in life.	People are so egoistic.
Would you like to give me a time out.	I do not want to know you.
I have to serve so many needs that I wonder how I will be able to serve my own needs.	This costs my business a lot of money.
Sometimes people wish for rest and order in a confusing world.	Broke people go on holidays.
Mutual giving from the heart includes our flora and fauna.	We have to protect the environment.
I observe that I am unable to get the needs met that my business partners require to say yea from the heart.	My bankers do not lend me the amount I asked them for.
Never disconnect from life, no matter who you are talking to.	Never ask rich people for money.
What do you need to say yes to our business partnering?	Hey, let's do business together.
Stop talking and get it done.	How much does it cost me?
How many of my needs are covered?	What is in it for me?

REFERENCES

1. Human Nature

   You find human nature in every existing library but also in the authentic connection with another human being. Throw the life-alienated communication away, live and celebrate life.

HALLO LIFE

Welcome to my World

The World of

MILLIONAIRE
HUMANS

www.ingramcontent.com/pod-product-compliance
Lightning Source LLC
LaVergne TN
LVHW020430080526
838202LV00055B/5110